The
Rhyme Riot

The Rhyme Riot

Poems chosen by
Gaby Morgan

Illustrated by
Jane Eccles

MACMILLAN CHILDREN'S BOOKS

For Nikki and Molly

First published 2002 by Macmillan Children's Books

This edition published 2003 by Macmillan Children's Books
a division of Macmillan Publishers Limited
20 New Wharf Road, London N1 9RR
Basingstoke and Oxford
www.panmacmillan.com

Associated companies throughout the world

ISBN 0 330 39900 4

3 5 7 9 8 6 4 2

A CIP catalogue record for this book is available from the British Library.

Typeset by SX Composing DTP, Rayleigh, Essex
Printed and bound in Great Britain
by Mackays of Chatham plc, Chatham, Kent.

Contents

A Plea from an Angel

'I want to be *different*!

I want to wear brown —

And strum on a banjo

And fly upside down . . .'

Trevor Harvey

South to North; 1965

I was born South of the river
down in the delta, beyond the bayou
lived in the swamps just off the High Street
London alligators snapping my ankles.

It was Bromley, Beckenham, Penge, Crystal
    Palace
where the kids said *wotcha*, ate bits of *cike*,
the land my father walked as a boy
the land his father walked before him.

I was rooted there, stuck in the clay
until we drove North, moved to Yorkshire
a land of cobbles, coal pits and coke works
forges and steel, fires in the sky.

Where you walked through fields around your
    village
didn't need three bus-rides to see a farm.

It was Mexbrough, Barnsley, Sprotbrough,
    Goldthorpe
I was deafened by words, my tongue struck
    dumb
gobsmacked by a language I couldn't speak in.

Ayop sithee, it's semmers nowt
What's tha got in thi snap, chaze else paze?
Who does tha supoort, Owls else Blades?
Dun't thee tha me, thee tha thi sen
Tha's a rate un thee, giz a spice?

Cheese and peas, sweets and football
I rolled in a richness of newfound vowels
words that dazed, dazzled and danced
out loud in my head until it all made sense
in this different country, far away
from where I was born, South of the river.

David Harmer

Paying His Respects

Great Grandad never talked
About the war.
'That,' he'd say with a sigh,
'That's over and done with.'

When I asked him
If the war was like the wars
In comics and in films,
He simply said,
'No, it was real.'

Every year
He got out his medals
And joined the parade
To the cenotaph,
Paying his respects.

John Foster

Escape Plan

As I, Stegosaurus,
stand motionless
in the museum
I am secretly planning
my escape.

At noon
Tyrannosaurus Rex
will cause a diversion
by wheeling around the museum's high ceilings
and diving at the curators and museum staff
while I
quietly slip out of the fire exit
and melt
into the London crowds.

Roger Stevens

Red Running Shoes

I wore some other girl's red running shoes
with real spikes like rose thorns under my foot.

I got into position: my limbs seriously tense,
one knee on the asphalt, one foot flat, all that.

I crouched over, hands down, like a predator
ready for prey; and took off, took flight

on the red running track, so fast I could be fear
running, a live fright, a chance vision.

My dark hair wild in the wind.
My arms pounding light years, thin air,
    euphoria.

I flew past in some other girl's red running shoes
round the red track, near the railway line.

I raced straight towards the future.
The past was left standing behind, waving.

I ran and ran; my feet became the land.
I couldn't tell if the ground was moving under
    my feet

shifting sand, or if I might ever just stop like a
    heartbeat.
It felt as if I could run for ever, hard pounding
    feet

until I ran into myself, years on
sat still, heavy, pasty forty, groaning, the streak
    lightning gone.

Jackie Kay

Thinking of You

Sometimes I think of you
the way that the thinnest
wisp of a cloud
teased out
to gauzy mist
drifts off across the blue,

but sometimes too
the dark sky loaded with thunder
presses down
like a slab of stone
which I lie under
thinking of you.

John Mole

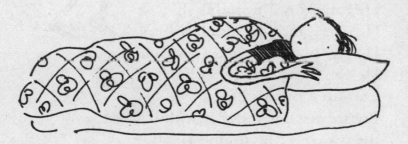

He Just Can't Kick It with His Foot

John Luke from our team
Is a goal-scoring machine
Phenomenally mesmerizing but . . .
The sport is called football
But his boots don't play at all
Cos he just can't kick it with his foot

He can skim it from his shin
He can spin it on his chin
He can nod it in the net with his nut
He can blow it with his lips
Or skip it off his hips
But he just can't kick it with his foot

With simplicity and ease
He can use his knobbly knees
To blast it past the keeper, both eyes shut
He can whip it up and flick it
Up with his tongue and lick it
But he just can't kick it with his foot

Overshadowing the best
With the power from his chest
Like a rocket from a socket he can put
The ball into the sack
With a scorcher from his back
But he just can't kick it with his foot

Baffling belief
With the ball between his teeth
He can dribble his way out of any rut
Hypnotize it with his eyes
Keep it up on both his thighs
But he just can't kick it with his foot

From his shoulder to his nose
He can juggle it and pose
With precision and incision he can cut
Defences straight in half
With a volley from his calf
But he just can't kick it with his foot

He can keep it off the deck
Bounce the ball upon his neck
With his ball control you should see him strut
He can flap it with both ears
To loud applause and cheers
But he just can't kick it with his foot

He can trap it with his tum
Direct it with his bum
Deflect it just by wobbling his gut
When he's feeling silly
He can even use his ankle
But he just can't kick it with his foot.

Paul Cookson

Staff Meeting

The teachers have gathered in private to talk
About their collections of left-over chalk –
Bits that are rare, bits they just like,
And fragments they've saved just in case there's
   a strike.
One has a blue that you don't often see,
Another a remnant from nineteen-oh-three.

They've thousands of pieces in boxes and tins,
Each sorted and counted with tweezers and
    pins.
And when all their best bits have been on
    display,
They'll take them home carefully, and lock them
    away.

Nick Toczek

The Music Lesson Rap

I'm the bongo kid,
I'm the big-drum-beater,
I'm the click-your-sticks,
I'm the tap-your-feeter.
When the lesson starts,
When we clap our hands,
Then it's me who dreams
Of the boom-boom bands,
And it's me who stamps,
And it's me who yells
For the biff-bang gong,
Or the ding-dong bells,
Or the cymbals (large),
Or the cymbals (small),
Or the tubes that chime
Round the bash-crash hall,
Or the tambourine,
Or the thunder-maker –
But all you give me
Is the sssh-sssh shaker!

Clare Bevan

Reincarnation

I'm
putting my name down
to come back
a cat
like our Cleo,

snooze
the whole of my next life away,
letting my pride and joy,
my tail,
find the warmest places,

that corner of the garden
where the sun lingers
round the roots of the laburnum,

that spot on the landing
where hot water pipes run
under the carpet;

whenever I want to
I'll stretch myself,
arching my back ecstatically,

dig my fine claws into
the bedside rug,
a plump cushion, someone's lap;

I'll go mooching and mousing
by the light of the moon

and come in any old time I like!

You can guarantee
someone will always
be there

to feed me, stroke me,
make me purr.

Matt Simpson

A Proper Poet

Today we have a real-live poet in school –
This gentleman who's standing next to me.
I must say when I met him in the entrance,
He was not as I imagined he would be.

I'd always thought that poets were tall and wan,
With eyes as dark and deep as any sea,
So when I saw this jolly little man,
He didn't seem a proper poet to me.

The poets I've seen in pictures dress in black
With velvet britches buttoned at the knee,
So when I saw the T-shirt and the jeans,
He didn't look a proper poet to me.

I've read that famous poets are often ill,
And die consumptive deaths on a settee.
Well I'd never seen a healthier looking man
He just didn't look a proper poet to me.

My favourite poems are by Tennyson and Keats.
This modern stuff is not my cup of tea,
So when I heard our poet was keen on rap
He didn't sound a proper poet to me.

Well, I'm certain that we'll all enjoy his poems
And listen – after all we've paid his fee –
I hope that they're in verses and they rhyme
For that is proper poetry – to me.

Gervase Phinn

Canary

The dome of his head
Is round as an egg.
His skull as delicate as shell,
The bones inside his little body
Fine as pins.

I can spread his yellow wings
Like feather fans,
But he won't sing.
Not again. Not ever.
He is light as dust
And I must bury him.

His bright body
Like sunshine in a box
Deep in the shade
Of dark rhododendrons.
Muffled. Silent.
In the soft black soil.

Jan Dean

Betrayal

Like rollerblades, we make a pair.
Watch us practise; with such flair
Pavements fly beneath our feet
In this kingdom of concrete
The original polyurethane pals
Surfing down suburban hills
Gossip, giggle, God it's great
To hang out with my best mate.

But my best matc's become a spy,
Sold my secrets. I blink my eye
And he has gone to the other side.
The Gang ride by; I try to hide,
Cover my feelings with concrete
As pavements fly beneath my feet
I climb the hills of hurt and hate
To get away from my best mate.

Andrew Fusek Peters

Moon Song

Why do I eye the moon
as it shines so bright in the still night sky?

Why do I sigh and swoon
as the clouds drift softly, silently by?

Why does it pull at my heart
there through the pane in the cold blue dawn?

Why does this longing start
there in myself where the song is born?

Tony Mitton

Fancy Free

It was the time of daffodils
And I fancy free
So free; as free
As birds that home to nests
Propelled by the season:
And how free are they?

It was the time of the autumn crocus
And I free, fancy free
Heart so free, as free
As leaves whirling down from trees
Unattached, loosed on the air:
And how free are they?

Jenny Joseph

A Feather from an Angel

Anton's box of treasures held
a silver key and a glassy stone,
a figurine made of polished bone
and a feather from an angel.

The figurine was from Borneo,
the stone from France or Italy,
the silver key was a mystery
but the feather came from an angel.

We might have believed him if he'd said,
'The feather fell from a bleached white crow',
but he always replied, 'It's an angel's, I know,
a feather from an angel.'

We might have believed him if he'd said,
'An albatross let the feather fall',
but he had no doubt, no doubt at all,
his feather came from an angel.

'I thought I'd dreamt him one night,' he'd say,
'but in the morning I knew he'd been there;
he left a feather on my bedside chair,
a feather from an angel.'

And it seems that all my life I've looked
for the sort of belief that nothing could shift,
something simple and precious as Anton's gift,
a feather from an angel.

Brian Moses

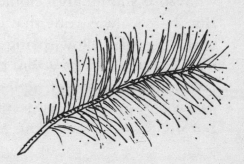

On the Laptop of the Little Lambs

On the laptop of the little lambs
it is written:
do not stray too far from your mother,
do not try to squeeze under the fence,
do not go near dogs.

Most cold March mornings
and each Easter in April,
the lambs gather in threes and fours
to power up their laptops
and read these simple instructions,
do not stray too far from your mother,
do not try to squeeze under the fence,
do not go near dogs.

The lambs know
what they should and should not do.
But there's always one that lets things slip
and while the yellow spring sun
tries its quiet best to warm the world,
one lamb wanders off, squeezes under the fence
and meets up with an Alsatian.

Perhaps we need bigger and bolder letters
on the laptop of the little lambs:

**do not stray too far from your
    mother,**
**do not try to squeeze under the
    fence,**
do not go near dogs.

It's hard to fix a fault in life's software.

John Rice

The Music I Like

The music I like
Is very special music.

At this moment,
For instance,

I'm listening to the washing machine
Slowing down,

As the gerbil rattles
In its cage,

And my wife runs
Up the stairs

And my next-door neighbour
Cuts his grass.

Music, very special music.
Just listen . . .

Ian McMillan

Trees on Parade

The trees are on fire! The trees are on fire!
Call for the fire brigade!
The branches are blazing, the canopies flaming
All along the colonnade.
The trees are on fire, the trees are on fire,
That's the end of the trees, I'm afraid.

Don't worry, they're not burning,
It's just the leaves turning,
In time for their autumn parade.

The trees are all sparkling! The trees are all
    sparkling!
The sweet chestnut, the aspen and lime
Are laced with fine threads, and delicate beads
Of silver and diamonds and I'm
More or less certain, that gossamer curtain's
Made by craftsmen who worked overtime.

Oh, it's the rime and the dew,
On the chestnut and yew,
Those jewels are not worth a dime.

The trees are all dressed up, the trees are all
    dressed up,
It's a most peculiar thing,
In bright green and pink, the cherry trees,
    I think,
Are preparing to go to a wedding,
Is that music I hear, from the boughs of the
    pear,
Have you heard of trees that could sing?

Those are buds and leaves waking,
And birds merry-making,
It always happens in spring.

The trees are in trouble, the trees are in trouble,
They're covered with small coloured balls,
Orange and green, russet and tangerine,
That old tree down by the stone wall
And the one by the road, are bending under
    their load,
I don't think they look happy at all.

Those are fruit on the boughs,
If you chase off those cows
I can climb up and fill this holdall.

Valerie Bloom

The Wolf's Wife Speaks

He was always out and about.
First on the block
To be up at the crack of dawn
Sniffing the morning air.

Of course,
Pork was his favourite.
I tell you, he would go a long way
For a nice bit of crackling,
Or to catch a tasty piglet or two.

But in the end
It all got too much –
All that huffing and puffing
Up and down the den,
Muttering in his sleep
That he would blow the house down!

Something was wrong,
I could tell –
Something had put his nose
Out of joint.

He'd come home full of bravado,
Swaggering into the den,
Flashing me that wolfish grin –
All teeth and tongue –
Then he'd set about boasting,
Full of big talk about
blowing up another building.
It cut no ice with me.

The tell-tale signs were there –
Some days he'd get back
covered in straw,
hardly able to draw breath.
What he'd been up to,
Lord alone knows . . .

Well it all came to a head,
When late one afternoon –
He shot back in,
With his fur singed.

I had to laugh –
He looked so funny,
Stood there with his bare bottom
Red as a radish.
Talk about coming home
With his tail between his legs!
Where he'd been – I can't imagine.
He never said.

He stays more at home now.
Well, he's prone to bronchitis –
This time of year you can hear him coming,
Poor old thing –
Wheezing and puffing,
Hardly able to draw breath.

We don't talk about it –
And he's right off pork!
If you ask me,
It's all been
a bit of a blow
To his ego.

Pie Corbett

The Blacksmith

Got tired of all the noise –
The hammer's clashing beat,
Got tired of all the smoke –
The spark-showers and the heat,
Got tired of all the beasts –
Their stamp-stamp and their stare,
Got tired of all the sweat
And the red coals' glare.

Went down to the sea one day,
Heard the water sing,
Took off all his clothes,
His apron, everything,
Waded out and dived
With seals and porpoises,
Set up shop on a reef to make
Shoes for sea horses.

Richard Edwards

Lullaby

If I could write some music for the rain
To play upon your nursery window pane
You'd sleep the sounder for its lullaby
And it would sing more tunefully than I.

If I could teach the clock to tell you tales
Of unicorns and ships with silver sails
You'd never hear the story fail and die
For clocks don't tend to nod as much as I.

If I could knit the shadows into shawls,
Unpick bad dreams and wind them into balls,
We'd throw them through the window at the sky,
Then pull the darkness round us, you and I.

Sue Cowling

After Giacometti
(1901-1966)

Look –
this
man
is
very
very
thin
but
still
standing
up –
and
I
for
one
believe
that
is
some
sort of
achievement.

note: Giacometti
was a sculptor who
sculpted very thin
people.

Fred Sedgwick

Icy Fingers

Despite the cold
A line of old trees
Playing with the moon

Tossing it
From one to the other
Never missing a catch.

Roger McGough

The Magic Show

After a feast of sausage rolls,
Sandwiches of various meats,
Jewelled jellies, brimming bowls
Of chocolate ice and other treats,
We children played at Blind Man's Buff,
Hide-and-Seek, Pin-the-Tail-on-Ned,
And then – when we'd had just enough
Of party games – we all were led
Into another room to see
The Magic Show. The wizard held
A wand of polished ebony;
His white-gloved, flickering hands compelled
The rapt attention of us all.
He conjured from astonished air
A living pigeon and a fall
Of paper snowflakes; made us stare
Bewildered, as a playing card –
Unlike a leopard – changed its spots
And disappeared. He placed some starred
And satin scarves in silver pots,

Withdrew them as plain bits of rag,
Then swallowed them before our eyes.
But soon we felt attention flag
And found delighted, first surprise
Had withered like a wintry leaf;
And, when the tricks were over, we
Applauded, yet felt some relief,
And left the party willingly.
'Good night', we said, 'and thank you for
The lovely time we've had.' Outside
The freezing night was still. We saw
Above our heads the slow clouds stride
Across the vast, unswallowable skies;
White, graceful gestures of the moon,
The stars intent and glittering eyes,
And, gleaming like a silver spoon,
The frosty path to lead us home.
Our breath hung blossoms on unseen
Boughs of air as we passed there,
And we forgot that we had been
Pleased briefly by that conjuror,
Could not recall his tricks, or face,
Bewitched and awed, as now we were,
By magic of the commonplace.

Vernon Scannell

Singing with Recordings

We lick same stick of ice cream.
We tickle each other to screams.

Just as each catches the ball from each
we leap the other's back with a touch.

Knowing each one's hating and loving
we rush with whispers to our hiding.

We get buried in the sand together.
We sing with recordings together.

We blow that one lucky-dip whistle.
We share our one used-tissue.

Not unlike two head-to-tail horses
there, standing in the rain
we get showered together again and again.

James Berry

Football in the Rain

It's drizzling.
'Football practice!'
'Oh, sir!
Do we have to?'
We look hopefully at Mr Tomkins,
But he says,
'Don't be such babies!'
So out we go.

It's raining harder.
We all start to moan,
'Can't we go in, sir?
We're getting soaked!'
But Mr Tomkins is not impressed.
'Tough. Get on with it!'
He says, putting up his umbrella
And retreating to the touchline.

It's coming down in buckets.
There are puddles all over the pitch,
And the rest is just mud.
Eddy falls over,
And comes up looking like
The Mud Monster from Hell.
We all start falling over,
Because we all want to look like that.

It's really chucking it down.
Mr Tomkins gets rain in his whistle.
Gurgle-gurgle-PHEEEP!
'Everybody in!'
We start moaning again.
'Oh, sir!
Do we have to?'

David Orme

Claws

If my cat
were a fish, he'd be a shark.
A big shark.
A big, mean shark.
A Great White Shark.

But he's not a fish.
He's a cat.
A big cat.
A big, mean cat.
A Great White Cat

who cruises the neighbourhood
terrorizing any creature
he happens to meet.

Birds wing away
when he prowls the gardens.
Other cats scat
when he struts his stuff
and even dogs make sure
they're somewhere else
when he's around.

He's rough. He's tough.
He's terrible to behold.
More terrible
than any tiger.

Sometimes he disappears
for days and days
and days

but just when
I start to think
I'll never see him again

in he strolls
pushing through the cat-flap
as if he's never been away

and he jumps up
into my lap
and curls himself
around himself

and falls asleep
purring like a Porsche
while I stroke him
and stroke him

and tell him
over and over again
that he's

the Best Cat
in the Whole Universe.

Tony Langham

Summer Farm

The mud cakes dry in the farmyard
The clouds have died a death
The lane shimmers like water
The air is holding its breath.

The dogs fall asleep to the music
Of cruising bumble bees
And the cows stand still as statues
As the stream slides past their knees.

Gareth Owen

The First Bit

I love the first bit of the morning,
The bit of the day that no one has used yet,
The part that is so clean
You must wipe your feet before you walk out
    into it.
The bit that smells like rose petals and cut grass
And dampens your clothes with dew.

If you go out you will bump into secrets,
Discover miracles usually covered by bus fumes.
You will hear pure echoes, whispers and
    scuttling.

I love the first bit of the morning
When the sun has only one eye open
And the day is like a clean shirt,
Uncreased and ready to put on;
The part that gets your attention
By being so quiet.

Coral Rumble